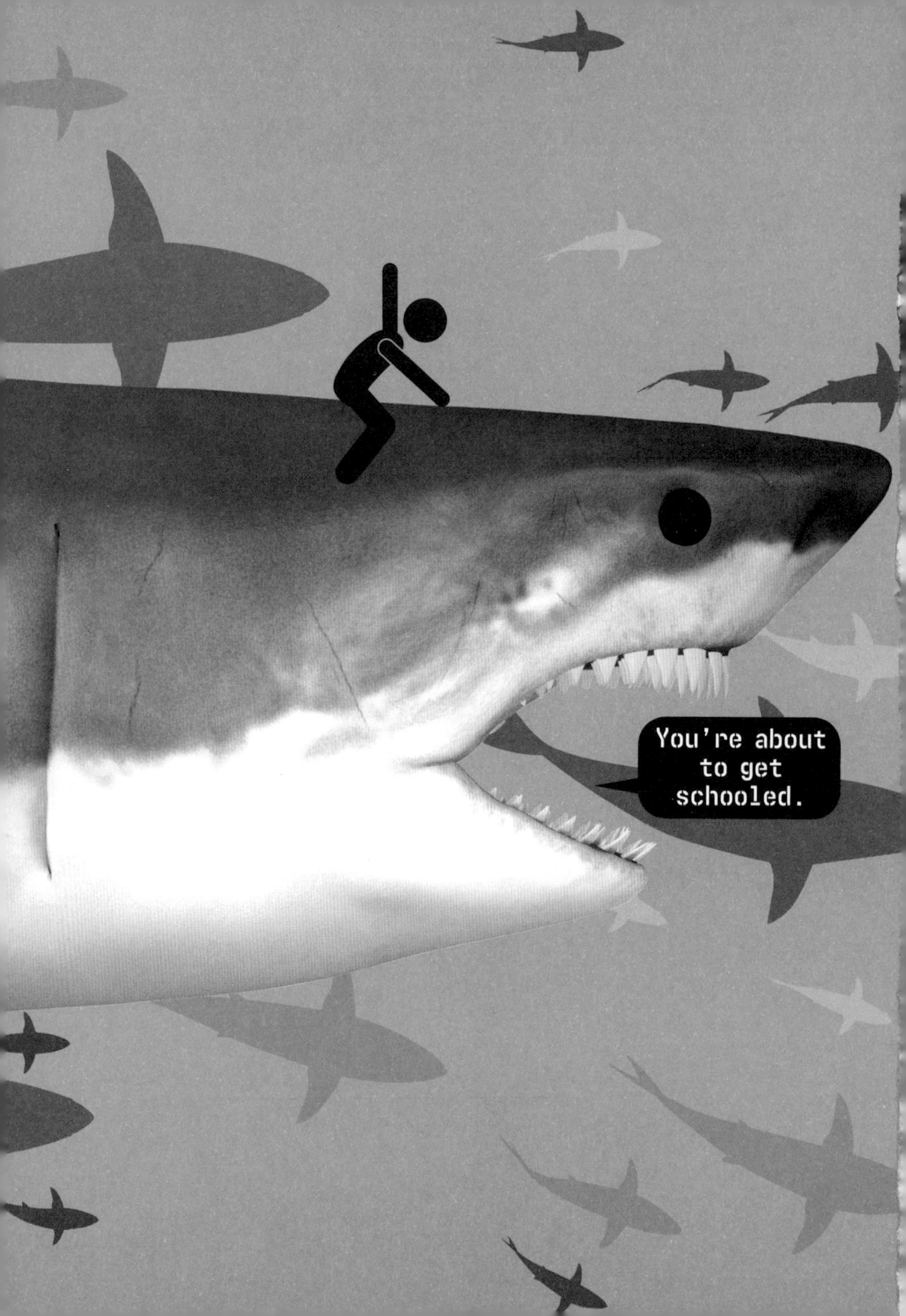
You're about to get schooled.

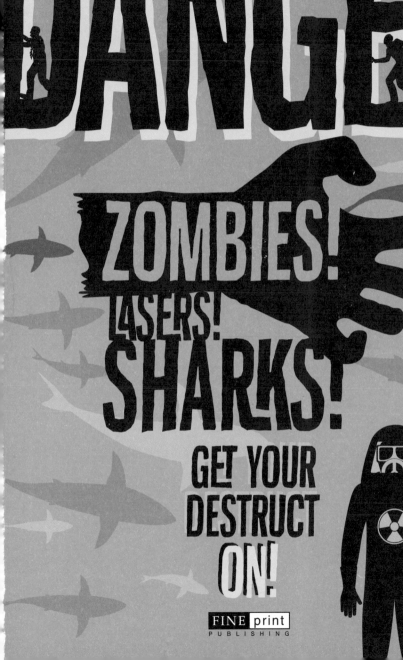

DANGER

ZOMBIES!
LASERS!
SHARKS!

GET YOUR DESTRUCT ON!

FINE print
PUBLISHING

DANGER

ZOMBIES!
LASERS!
SHARKS!

CREATED BY
MICKEY & CHERYL GILL

FINE print
PUBLISHING

Fine Print Publishing Company
P.O. Box 916401
Longwood, Florida 32791-6401

Created in the USA & Printed in China
This book is printed on acid-free paper.

ISBN 978-1-892951-81-6

2 3 5 7 9 10 8 6 4 1

WARNING   WARNING   WARNING   WARNING   WARNING

CLASSIFIED
DOCUMENTS
PROPERTY OF:

Name

TOP SECRET

DANGER DANGER DANGER DANGER WARNING

WARNING WAR... DANGER DANGE

A GOVERNMENT ORGANIZATION HAS RECRUITED YOU AS A SPECIAL AGENT. THE ORGANIZATION'S HEADQUARTERS [HQ] NEEDS HELP WITH:

☞ ZOMBIE SWARMS

☞ REMOTE-CONTROLLED SHARKS

☞ UNAUTHORIZED LASER WEAPON USE

☞ UNUSUAL THREATS TO NATIONAL SECURITY

FIND CLASSIFIED DOCUMENTS, MISSION ASSIGNMENTS, AND COVERT OPERATIONS.

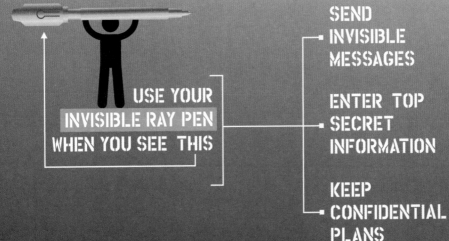

USE YOUR INVISIBLE RAY PEN WHEN YOU SEE THIS

SEND INVISIBLE MESSAGES

ENTER TOP SECRET INFORMATION

KEEP CONFIDENTIAL PLANS

WARNING WARNING WARNING WAR RNING WARNING WARNING WARNING WAR

DANGER

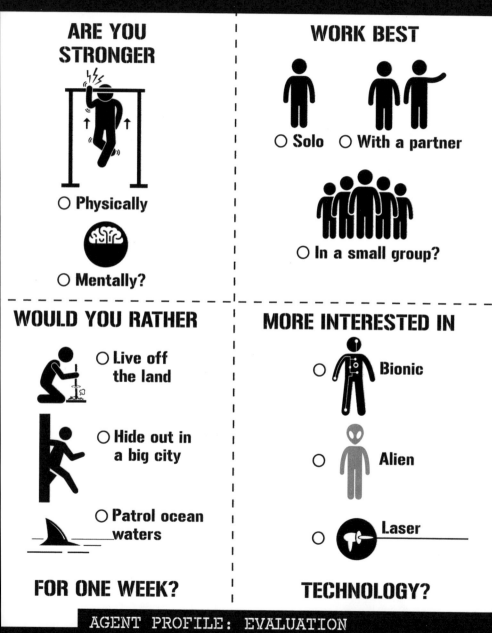

HOW ARE YOUR COMPUTER SKILLS?
O OK   O Great   O Off-the-charts awesome

LONGEST YOU'VE GONE WITHOUT TALKING?
O 1   O 5   O More than 5 hour(s)

HOW LONG CAN YOU BE PERFECTLY STILL?
O 30 Minutes   O 1 Hour   O More than 1 hour

HOW DO YOU FEEL ABOUT A SUIT AND TIE?
O Not good at all   O Fine   O Great

HOW DO YOU LOOK IN DARK SUNGLASSES?
O OK   O Amazing   O Swag-tastic!

WHICH COULD YOU HANDLE?

O **Zombie mob**

O **Circling sharks**

O **Laser weapon in the wrong hands**

TOP SECRET: RETIN

A SPECIAL AGENCY
WITHIN THE GOVT.
ORGANIZATION USES
**RETINA
SCANNERS**
AT EVERY ENTRY TO
IDENTIFY PEOPLE.
EACH SCANNER
ANALYZES THE
UNIQUE PATTERN
OF BLOOD VESSELS
ON THE BACK OF
THE EYEBALL.

YOUR PERSONAL
INFO WILL FLASH
UP ON A SCREEN
FOR REVIEW
BEFORE A DOOR
OPENS.

COMPLETE THIS
INFORMATION ABOUT
YOU FOR AGENCY
RECORDS.

YOUR AGENT NAME

HEIGHT/WEIGHT

LENGTH OF SECOND TOE

RECOGNITION 👁

| AUTHENTICATION

FAVORITE MEAT

LAST THING YOU ATE ON A STICK

WEIRDEST THING YOU'VE EVER DONE

HEAD
Main target. Blow to brain takes zombie down.

BITE OR KISS
Transmits zombie virus. But who would kiss a zombie?

gaaahhh

nooo

STRENGTH
There are two theories. They're either very strong or don't know when to let go. Avoid their grasp.

Does not feel pain.

RAGGED CLOTHING
Dead giveaway that someone is a zombie. It's a zombie's signature style.

INEFFICIENT LEGS
Not good at sprinting. Rare "runner" zombies are exceptions.

ZOMBIES IN AREA
STAY ALERT

SWARM OR MOB
Terms used to describe a group of zombies.

BRAIN

Frontal lobe
(tastes like Key lime pie)

Parietal lobe
(tastes like candy apples)

Occipital lobe
(tastes like spinach)

Zombies want living people's brains.

Zombies do not use full brainpower. This works in your favor.

Temporal lobe
(tastes like blueberry muffin)

Pons

Cerebellum

Medulla oblongata

Spinal cord

ZOMBIE-LIKE BEINGS

MUMMIES
Previously living beings are well preserved on purpose or by accident.
Do not qualify as zombies.

VAMPIRES
These threats to society are not in a constant state of decay.
Do not qualify as zombies.

PUBLIC E

YOU MUST TRAIL THESE EXTRA-THREATENING ZOMBIES. GIVE THEM CODE NAMES TO USE WHEN COMMUNICATING WITH AGENTS.

USE YOUR INVISIBLE RAY PEN

CODE NAME

CODE NAME

I'm on the heels of Fingerless Fred and Rot-Face Boy.

ZOMBIE SWARM SURVIVAL: TRAILIN

EMY NO. 1
(& 2,3,4,&5)

CODE NAME

CODE NAME

CODE NAME

YOU NEED TO BE PREPARED WHEN F
DISGUSTING PACKS OF ZOMBIES. MA
EVERYTHING MUST

WHAT YOU NEED TO
LIVE (AND NOT DIE FROM DEHYDRATION & STARVATION)

- ✓ WATER
- ✓ FOOD THAT WON'T SPOIL

WHAT WOULD YOU LIKE TO PACK?

_____

_____

- ✓ SOAP & TOWELS
- ✓ FIRST AID SUPPLIES
- ✓ TOOLS & SUPPLIES

WHAT DO YOU THINK YOU'LL NEED?

_____

_____

OWING, CHASING, OR RUNNING FROM
SURE YOU HAVE PROPER SUPPLIES.
IN THIS BACKPACK.

WHAT YOU NEED TO
LIVE (AND NOT DIE FROM
BOREDOM WHEN YOU'RE
NOT RUNNING FOR YOUR LIFE)

(✓) FUN STUFF TO
AMUSE YOU

[WHAT WOULD YOU PACK?]

_ _

_ _

_ _

_ _

_ _

_ _

_ _

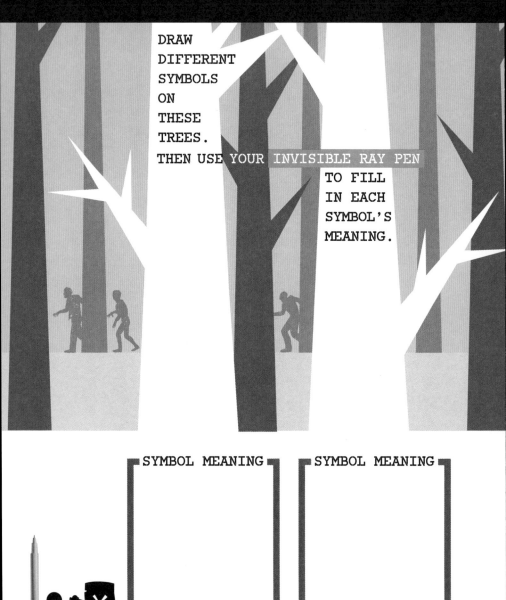

DRAW
DIFFERENT
SYMBOLS
ON
THESE
TREES.
THEN USE YOUR INVISIBLE RAY PEN
TO FILL
IN EACH
SYMBOL'S
MEANING.

SYMBOL MEANING

SYMBOL MEANING

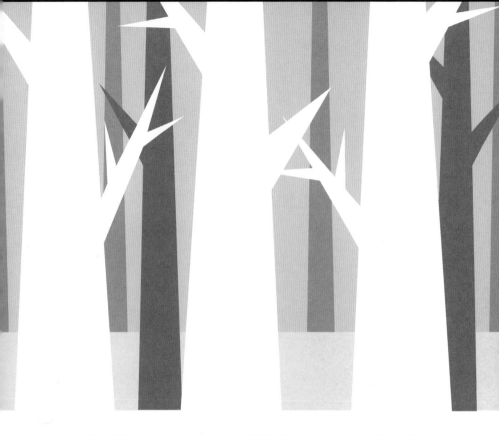

SYMBOL MEANING SYMBOL MEANING SYMBOL MEANING

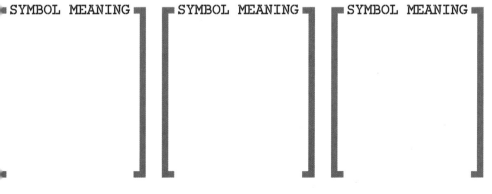

CHOOSE THREE PEOPLE TO WEAR ZOMBIE DISGUISES WITH YOU.

WHAT WOULD MAKE THEM AMAZING ZOMBIES?

USE YOUR INVISIBLE RAY PEN
TO WRITE THEIR NAMES.
KEEP IT CONFIDENTIAL.

SKILLS THAT WOULD MAKE
THEM AWESOME ZOMBIES

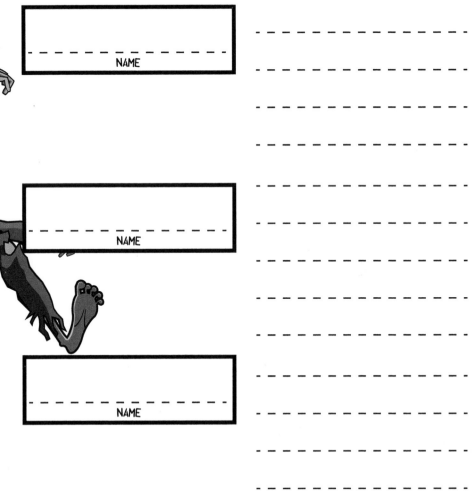

NAME

NAME

NAME

TOP SECRET: z.y.

HQ'S LABORATORY TECHS NEED YOUR [
YOU NEED REALLY GROSS INGREDIENTS
TO FIGHT THE VIRUS.

LABEL BOTTLES WITH GROSS INGREDIENT

...TIDOTE ☠

...CONCOCTING A ZOMBIE VIRUS ANTIDOTE.

> PREPARE
> BY MIXING
> INGREDIENTS

> A REMEDY THAT STOPS
> OR CONTROLS THE
> EFFECTS OF A POISON

...OR LAB TECHS TO COMBINE AND TEST.

IN CASE ZOMBIE SWARMS TU
YOU'LL NEED A S

USE A PENCIL TO MAP OUT AN ESCAPE ROUTE FROM YOUR
HOME TO A SECURE PLACE UNDERGROUND OR HIGH UP IN TOWN.

INTO A ZOMBIE APOCALYPSE,
PLACE TO HIDE.

TRACE OVER YOUR MAP WITH YOUR INVISIBLE RAY PEN. THEN
ERASE YOUR PENCIL SKETCH. NOW ONLY YOU KNOW THE LOCATION.

bies...

TOP SECRET PART

SECRET AGENT R59-2 HAS BEEN ASSIGNED TO YOU.
HQ REQUIRES CODE NAMES FOR YOUR
NEW PARTNERSHIP.

AGENT PROFILE: PARTNER CODE NAMES

COMBINE WORDS FROM EACH LIST TO CREATE A SECRET AGENT DUO NAME.

BLOCK

PEANUT BUTTER

BLACK

BISCUITS

HAMMER

DIP

BACON

THUNDER

HOT DOG

SOUR CREAM

SOCKS

LOCKED

BATMAN

ROUGH

DOWN

BOW

SKULL

DIRTY

CROSSBONES

READY

WHITE

ARROW

CHIPS

LOADED

STINKY

CHOCOLATE

BANANA

ONIONS

HAMBURGER

BLUE

ROBIN

GRAVY

JELLY

HONEY

EGGS

NAILS

LIGHTNING

TACKLE

_ _ _ _ _ _ _ _ & _ _ _ _ _ _ _ _

NEW SECRET AGENT DUO NAME

CONFIDENTIAL: DISGUIS

EVERY AGENT'S UNDERCOVER DISGUISE MUST BE KEPT ON FILE, LOCKED AWAY IN A SECURE, SECRET VAULT.

DRAW YOUR DISGUISE WITH YOUR INVISIBLE RAY PEN

YOU WILL ALSO NEED AN

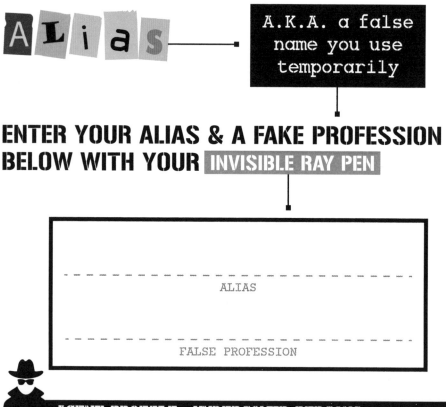

A.K.A. a false name you use temporarily

ENTER YOUR ALIAS & A FAKE PROFESSION BELOW WITH YOUR INVISIBLE RAY PEN

ALIAS

FALSE PROFESSION

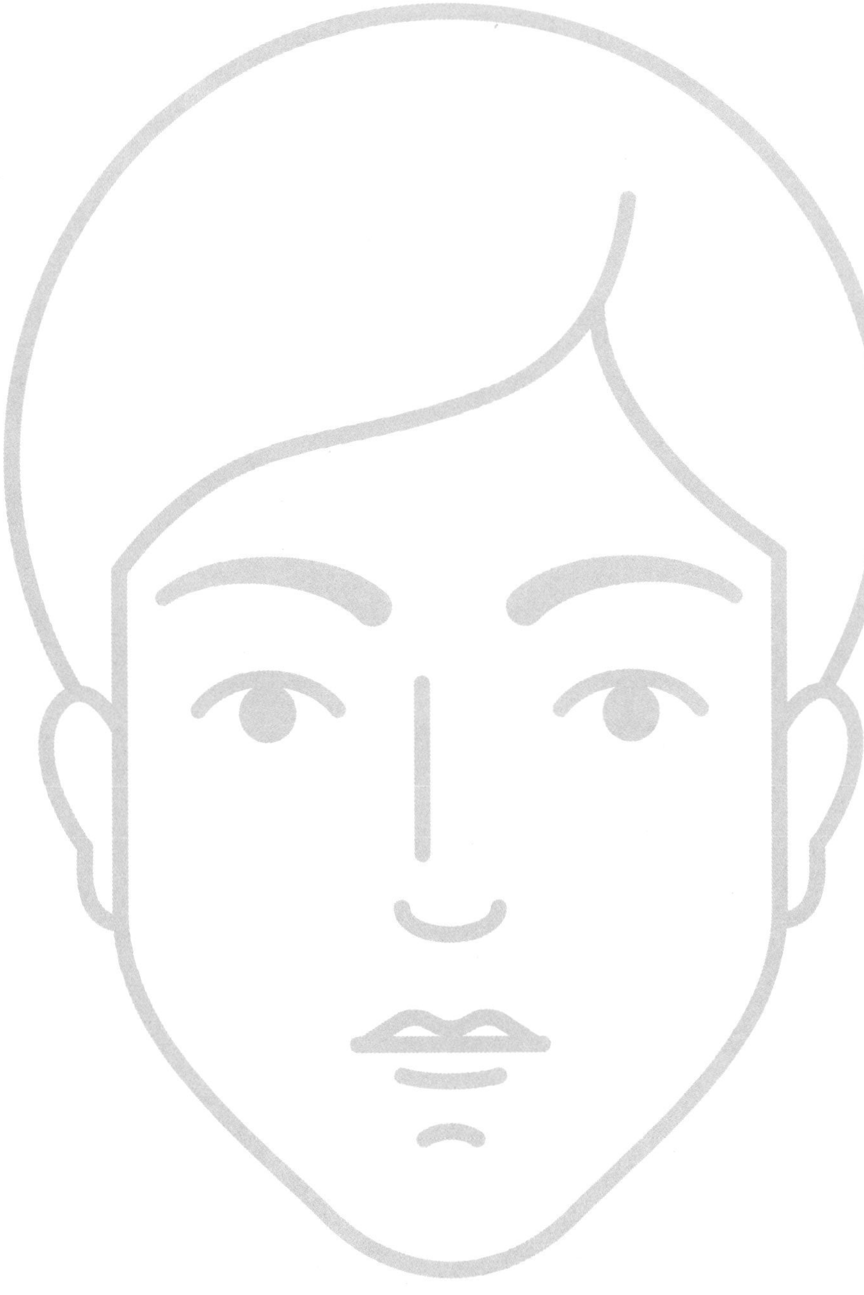

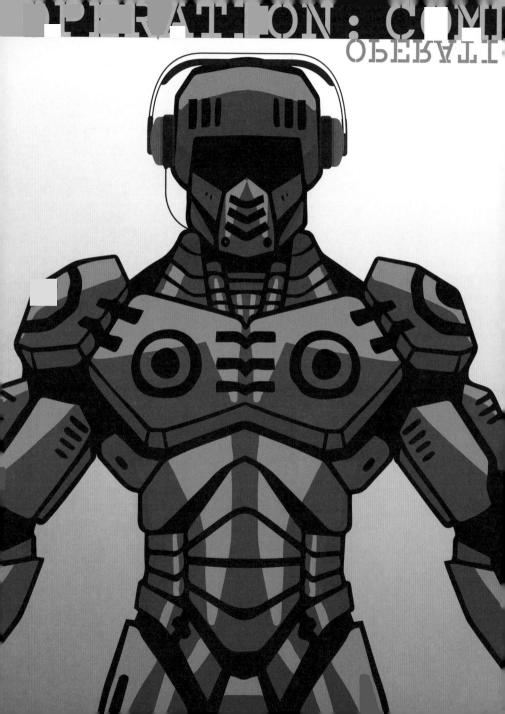

You should have some awesome tunes
as your background music when battling
zombies, cyborg sharks, & other
dangerous threats to society.

Create a playlist of songs
for taking on —

ZOMBIES

SONG

ARTIST

SONG

ARTIST

SONG

ARTIST

SONG

ARTIST

CYBORG SHARKS

SONG

ARTIST

SONG

ARTIST

SONG

ARTIST

SONG

ARTIST

CLASSIFIED: CASE NO. DX09

YOU BARELY ESCAPED A LEAGUE OF FRIGHTENIN

DRAW THEM BELOW WITH YOUR INVISIBLE RAY PEN
[THE PUBLIC MUST BE KEPT IN THE DARK.]

NKNOWN CREATURES.
UNDERCOVER AGENTS NEED A DESCRIPTION OF THEM.

LASER INTEL.

LIGHT AMPLIFICATION BY STIMULATED EMISSION OF RADIATION

STRONGEST SOURCE OF LIGHT CREATED BY MAN

COLOR

Lasers exist in different colors such as red, green, yellow, and blue.

LASER USES

- Missile guidance
- Holograms
- Cutting, welding, heating
- Target destruction
- Sensor disabler

Lasers can be hazardous to your health. Do not shine at people, animals, or any reflective surface. Highly dangerous.

Can damage

yikessss

LASERS OF THE FUTURE

The military is currently testing a laser weapon system that can disable a small drone, detonate a rocket-propelled grenade, and burn out the engine of an inflatable boat.

EXTERMINATE!

RAY GUN REGISTRATION

THE ORGANIZATION IS CUSTOMIZING A RAY GUN FOR YOU. IT'S A DEFENSIVE WEAPON, ONLY FOR EMERGENCIES.

CHOOSE UP TO

3
DIFFERENT RAYS FOR YOUR WEAPON OR REQUEST ADDITIONAL RAYS NOT LISTED.

☐ LASER BEAM

☐ FREEZE RAY

☐ PARTICLE BEAM

☐ PLASMA PULSE

☐ DISINTEGRATOR

☐ ENLARGENATOR

☐ GLOW-IN-THE-DARK PAINT

☐ HEAT RAY

☐ VAPORIZER

☐ SKITTLE SPRAY

☐ SHRINKINATOR

☐ HAIRY BACK RAY

☐ BABY POOP

☐ ENEMY DRONE DESTROYING

Get 'em Ronnie Ray Gun!

WARNING
IF YOU DO NOT USE YOUR RAY GUN RESPONSIBLY, IT WILL BE SEIZED AND LOCKED IN A VAULT.

LASER TECHNOLOGY: SELF DEFENSE

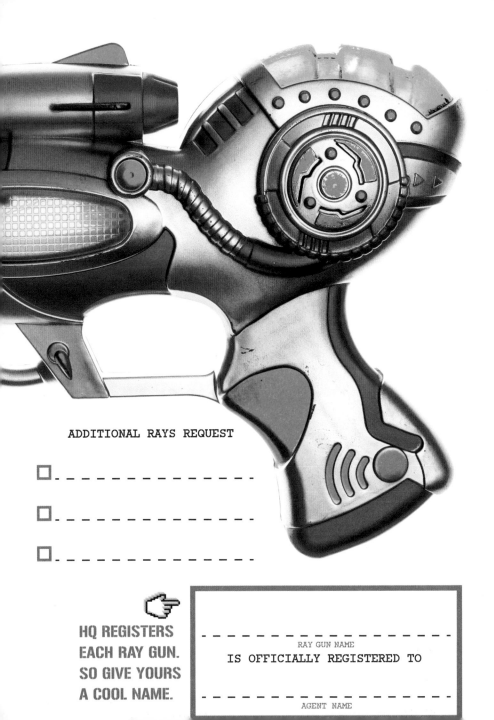

ADDITIONAL RAYS REQUEST

☐ _ _ _ _ _ _ _ _ _ _ _ _ _

☐ _ _ _ _ _ _ _ _ _ _ _ _ _

☐ _ _ _ _ _ _ _ _ _ _ _ _ _

HQ REGISTERS
EACH RAY GUN.
SO GIVE YOURS
A COOL NAME.

_ _ _ _ _ _ _ _ _ _ _ _ _
RAY GUN NAME
IS OFFICIALLY REGISTERED TO

_ _ _ _ _ _ _ _ _ _ _ _ _
AGENT NAME

TO PROTECT YOU FROM THE ENEMY, HEADQUARTERS NEEDS TO OUTFIT YOU WITH HIDDEN LASERS. MAKE LISTS OF WHERE YOU'D LIKE TECHS TO HIDE THE LASER DEVICES.

[INSIDE A BASEBALL CAP, REMOTE CONTROL, BOOK, ETC.]

[ON YOU]

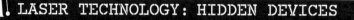

LASER TECHNOLOGY: HIDDEN DEVICES

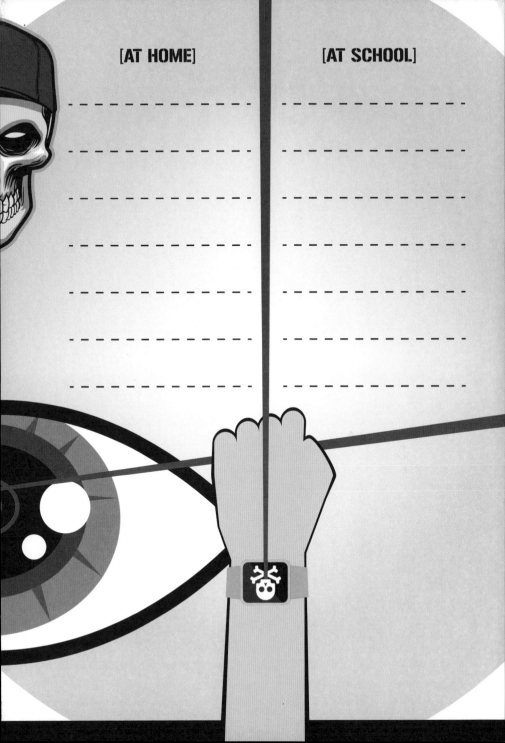

[AT HOME]

[AT SCHOOL]

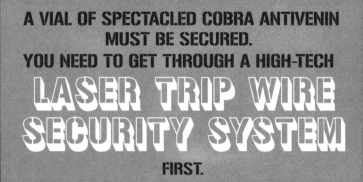

A VIAL OF SPECTACLED COBRA ANTIVENIN MUST BE SECURED.
YOU NEED TO GET THROUGH A HIGH-TECH
LASER TRIP WIRE SECURITY SYSTEM
FIRST.

LASER TECHNOLOGY: TRIP WIRE NAVIGATION TEST

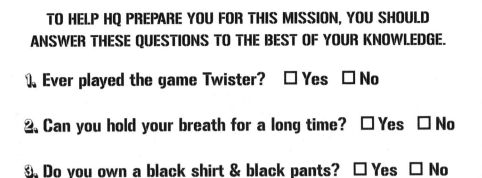

TO HELP HQ PREPARE YOU FOR THIS MISSION, YOU SHOULD ANSWER THESE QUESTIONS TO THE BEST OF YOUR KNOWLEDGE.

1. Ever played the game Twister? ☐ Yes ☐ No

2. Can you hold your breath for a long time? ☐ Yes ☐ No

3. Do you own a black shirt & black pants? ☐ Yes ☐ No

4. Are you careful? ☐ Yes ☐ No

5. Think you can lower yourself from the ceiling
with a rope? ☐ Yes ☐ No

6. Ever done the limbo? ☐ Yes ☐ No

7. Can you dive into a somersault? ☐ Yes ☐ No

8. Ever slid into a base? ☐ Yes ☐ No

9. Good at catching yourself before you trip or fall?
☐ Yes ☐ No

10. Can you do a backbend? ☐ Yes ☐ No

Turn upside down for test results.

— If you answered —

Mostly "yes" to questions, you're more than qualified for the mission.

About half "yes" and half "no", HQ will be following up to work with you.

Mostly "no" to questions, HQ will be reassigning you.

OPERATION: JA

AN EVIL SCIENTIST
IS ENGINEERING A
NEW UNDERWATER
CIVILIZATION WHERE
REMOTE-CONTROLLED
SHARKS RULE.

YOU AND YOUR
LASER-TRAINED
ROBO-SKELETON
MUST TAKE OUT
HIS RESEARCH
FACILITY.

AMMOGAWS-TECH TAKEDOWN

1. TAKE OUT THE FACILITY'S SECRET ESCAPE EXIT, CONTROL CENTER & SHARK TECHNOLOGY.

2. DO NOT HIT ANY MINIONS.

3. ONLY SHOOT THROUGH TWO OPEN WINDOWS. [IT MUST BE A SURPRISE.]

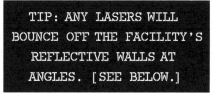

TIP: ANY LASERS WILL BOUNCE OFF THE FACILITY'S REFLECTIVE WALLS AT ANGLES. [SEE BELOW.]

DRAW UP A QUICK PLAN USING YOUR INVISIBLE RAY PEN AND A RULER. DRAW LASER PATHS ON THE FACILITY MAP. ----►

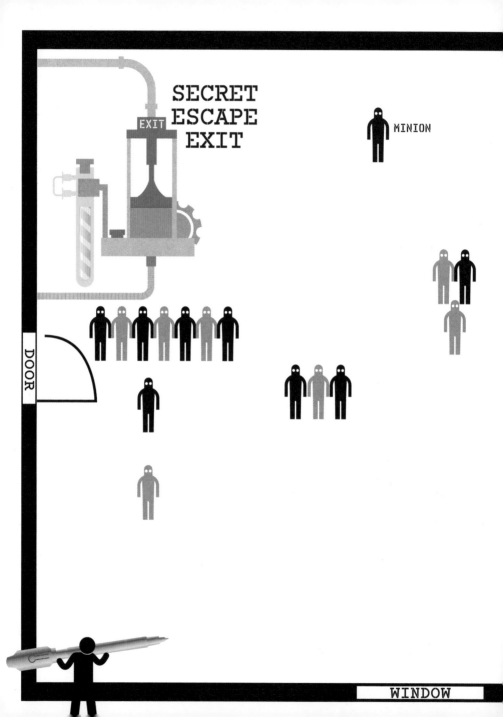

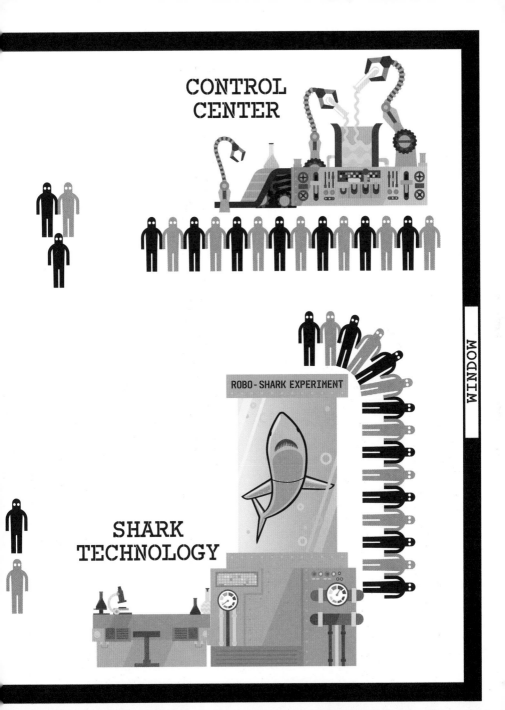

CONTROL
CENTER

ROBO-SHARK EXPERIMENT

SHARK
TECHNOLOGY

WINDOW

LANGUAGE !

"   "

IS CODE FOR

"THERE IS AN ENEMY AMONG US."

"   "

IS CODE FOR

"HE'S PACKING A LASER GUN."

"   "

IS CODE FOR

"CALL FOR BACKUP."

"   "

IS CODE FOR

"COVER ME FROM BEHIND."

"   "

IS CODE FOR

"TAKE HIM DOWN ON THE COUNT OF 3."

MISSIONS CAN BE EXTREMELY DANGEROUS FOR INNOCENT BYSTANDERS. YOU NEED TO BE ABLE TO EMPTY A ROOM FULL OF PEOPLE QUICKLY.

HELP THE AGENCY EQUIP YOUR GOVERNMENT-ISSUED WRISTWATCH WITH FEATURES THAT COULD CLEAR A ROOM. USE YOUR **INVISIBLE RAY PEN** TO FILL IN SPECIAL FEATURES.

10:42
Mon 12 feb   25°

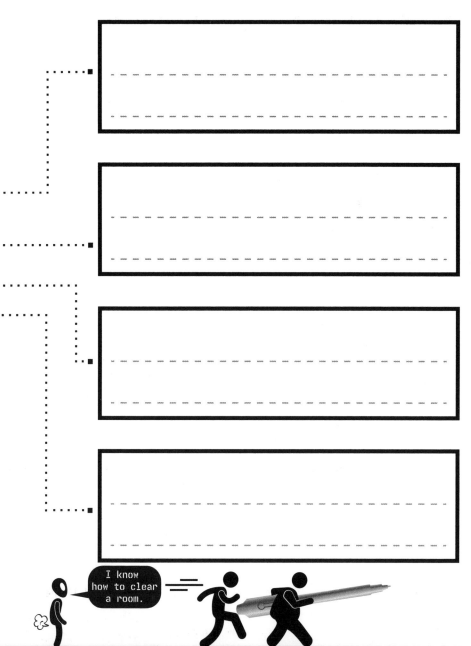

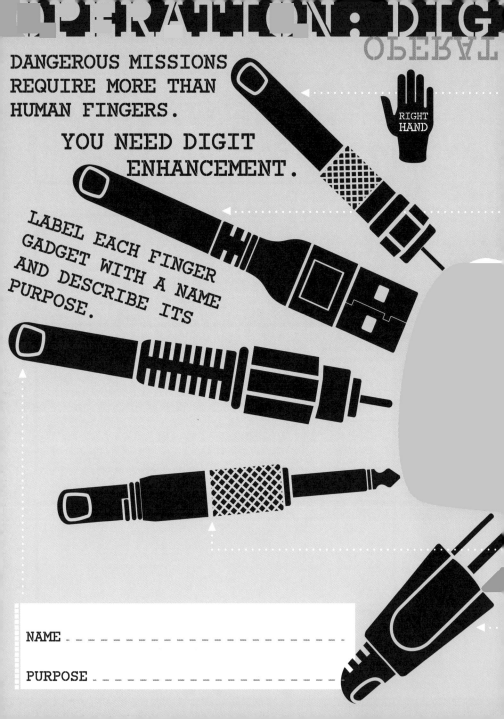

OPERATION DIGIT

DANGEROUS MISSIONS
REQUIRE MORE THAN
HUMAN FINGERS.

YOU NEED DIGIT
ENHANCEMENT.

RIGHT
HAND

LABEL EACH FINGER
GADGET WITH A NAME
AND DESCRIBE ITS
PURPOSE.

NAME _

PURPOSE _

NAME

PURPOSE

NAME

PURPOSE

NAME

PURPOSE

NAME

PURPOSE

OPERATION: DIG

OPERATION

NOW BUILD YOUR OWN LEFT HAND.
CREATE GADGETS, NAME THEM,
AND DESCRIBE PURPOSE.

LEFT
HAND

NAME _

PURPOSE _

NAME _

PURPOSE _

NAME _

_ _

PURPOSE _

_ _

NAME _

PURPOSE _

NAME _____

PURPOSE _____

HEADQUARTERS OUTPOST: EXTENSION SETUP

HEADQUARTERS

NEEDS YOUR HELP TRANSFORMING YOUR BEDROOM INTO A HQ OUTPOST.

1 SKETCH A PLAN OF YOUR BEDROOM (LIKE YOU'RE LOOKING AT IT FROM ABOVE) ON THE NEXT PAGE.

2 THEN USE YOUR `INVISIBLE RAY PEN` TO ADD THESE SECRET FEATURES [BELOW]. EACH ONE SHOULD BE HIDDEN UNDER A BED, IN A CLOSET, ETC.

CONTROL PANEL

ESCAPE HATCH DOOR

HIGH-ENERGY RAY GUN

TRANSPORTATION TUBE

MOTORCYCLE AND MOTORCYCLE BAY

Can I get
some chips?

BEWARE

CYBORG GREAT WHITE
Implanted with
artificial intelligence.
DANGER LEVEL: Code Orange

NUCLEAR-POWERED MAKO
Termination may lead
to worldwide destruction.
DANGER LEVEL: Code Red

ROBO-BULL SHARK
Remotely controlled
by humans.
DANGER LEVEL: Code Orange

SNOUT

SPIRACLE
Opening that draws in oxygenated
water in from above. Aids in
breathing.

ROWS OF RAZOR-
SHARP TEETH

GILL
SLITS

WARNING: LATERAL LINE
Senses vibrations & odor
plumes in the water.
Assists in detecting prey.

— FIRST
DORSAL FIN

CAUDAL FIN

SECOND
DORSAL FIN

PELVIC FIN

PECTORAL FIN

MEGALODON

WHALE SHARK

GREAT WHITE

SHARK GUT VIDEO RETRIEVAL

A shark has swallowed a special government agency's underwater camera. It contains video of enemy spy activity. The Feds need you to feed the shark food that will make him throw up (cashew milk, lima beans, whatever it takes).

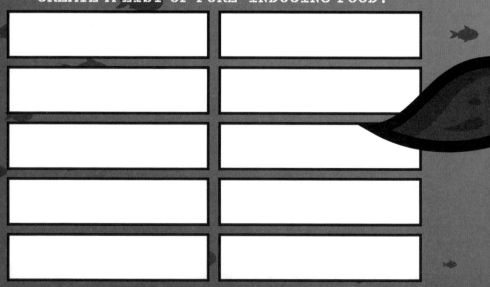

CREATE A LIST OF PUKE-INDUCING FOOD.

MISSION DK39SW:

SHARK WEAPONIZATION

AN INTERNATIONAL VILLAIN HAS
TRAINED SHARKS AT HIS COMMAND.

YOU MUST COUNTER HIM WITH
YOUR OWN SCHOOL.

HOW WILL YOU ARM THEM?
ADD NAMES & WEAPONIZATION DETAILS
TO THESE SHARK PROFILES.

NAME ------------------------------------

WEAPON: ------------------------------------

NAME ------------------------------------

WEAPON: ------------------------------------

NAME ------------------------------------

WEAPON: ------------------------------------

NAME ------------------------------------

WEAPON: ------------------------------------

MISSION D-99HC:
HAMMERHEAD/ANGLER CAPTURE

BACKGROUND: Two ocean fish have mutated into supervillains Hammerhead and Angler. They possess dangerous and very powerful human-like traits but still need saltwater to survive.

DATA: ANGLER

Attracts prey with fleshy growth on head.

Can swallow prey up to twice the size of its body.

Hammerhead uses angler to trick prey into swimming toward him.

DATA: HAMMERHEAD

Preys on fish, squid, octopus, crustaceans, & other sharks.

Self-taught karate and krav maga expert.

Salt feeds his superpowers. He is currently depleting the ocean of salt.

THERE IS CHATTER THAT A ROGUE BIOLOGIST IS CROSSING SHARKS WITH OTHER ANIMALS. TO CATCH A CRIMINAL LIKE HIM, YOU MUST THINK LIKE HIM.

SHARK ACTIVITY: GENETIC MODIFICATIONS

WHICH ANIMALS WOULD BE CRAZY, CREEPY, AND AWESOME TO COMBINE WITH SHARKS?

ANIMAL		NEW SPECIES
_ _ _ _ _ _ _ _ _ _ _ _	+ SHARK =	_ _ _ _ _ _ _ _ _ _ _ _
_ _ _ _ _ _ _ _ _ _ _ _	+ SHARK =	_ _ _ _ _ _ _ _ _ _ _ _
_ _ _ _ _ _ _ _ _ _ _ _	+ SHARK =	_ _ _ _ _ _ _ _ _ _ _ _
_ _ _ _ _ _ _ _ _ _ _ _	+ SHARK =	_ _ _ _ _ _ _ _ _ _ _ _
_ _ _ _ _ _ _ _ _ _ _ _	+ SHARK =	_ _ _ _ _ _ _ _ _ _ _ _
_ _ _ _ _ _ _ _ _ _ _ _	+ SHARK =	_ _ _ _ _ _ _ _ _ _ _ _
_ _ _ _ _ _ _ _ _ _ _ _	+ SHARK =	_ _ _ _ _ _ _ _ _ _ _ _
_ _ _ _ _ _ _ _ _ _ _ _	+ SHARK =	_ _ _ _ _ _ _ _ _ _ _ _
_ _ _ _ _ _ _ _ _ _ _ _	+ SHARK =	_ _ _ _ _ _ _ _ _ _ _ _
_ _ _ _ _ _ _ _ _ _ _ _	+ SHARK =	_ _ _ _ _ _ _ _ _ _ _ _
_ _ _ _ _ _ _ _ _ _ _ _	+ SHARK =	_ _ _ _ _ _ _ _ _ _ _ _

TOP SECRET: ROBO

A troop of robo-soldiers now report
to you for your most serious missions.

1. Use your INVISIBLE RAY PEN
   to write a one-word code name
   for the robot captain and
   his team.(Use these names
   during missions.)

2. Assign robots different
   skills (laser vision,
   invisibility cloaking,
   judo expert, etc.)

CODE NAME

- -

- -

SKILLS

- -

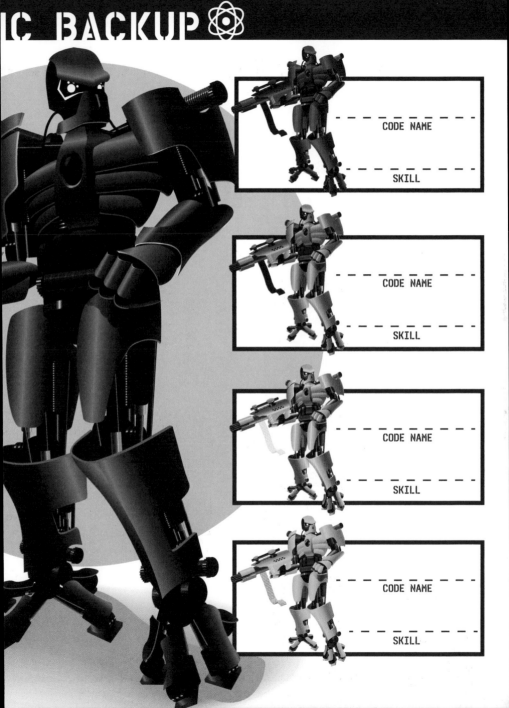

IC BACKUP

CODE NAME

SKILL

CODE NAME

SKILL

CODE NAME

SKILL

CODE NAME

SKILL

ENEMY **OPERATIVES** ARE CLONING US GOVERNMENT AGENTS.

People secretly employed in ESPIONAGE for a government.

Systematic use of spies to get political or military secrets.

IF THE FEDS BELIEVE THEY ARE WORKING WITH A CLONE OF YOU, THEY WILL ASK HIM QUESTIONS ONLY YOU WOULD KNOW.

AGENT PROFILE: HUMAN CLONE TESTING

INFORMATION

WRITE DOWN INFORMATION ABOUT YOURSELF THAT ONLY YOU KNOW. [YOUR FAMILY, FRIENDS, AND THE FLY ON THE WALL DO NOT KNOW THESE FACTS.] USE YOUR INVISIBLE RAY PEN

I climbed my neighbor's tree when I was five. My mom told me not to.

FACT #1

. . . .

. . . .

. . . .

FACT #2

. . . .

. . . .

. . . .

FACT #3

. . . .

. . . .

. . . .

SPECIAL AGENT K-9 WILL NOW BE YOUR COMPANION.
HE CAN ASSIST YOU DURING MISSIONS.

COMPLETE THIS PAPERWORK FOR HQ.

CHECK **5** FEATURES YOU WOULD LIKE PROGRAMMED INTO HIS CIRCUITRY.

- ☐ LASER VISION
- ☐ JIU-JITSU-TRAINED
- ☐ POTTY-TRAINED
- ☐ BIONIC HEARING
- ☐ SUPER SPEED
- ☐ SUPER CANINE SENSE OF SMELL
- ☐ SOUND BARRIER-BREAKING BARK
- ☐ OIL SLICK BOWEL MOVEMENTS
- ☐ DEFENSIVE NOXIOUS BREATH
- ☐ OTHER _ _ _ _ _ _ _ _ _ _ _ _ _ _ _ _
- ☐ OTHER _ _ _ _ _ _ _ _ _ _ _ _ _ _ _ _

HOW CAN AGENT K-9 HELP YOU ON MISSIONS?
WHAT EPIC FEATS COULD HE PERFORM?

- -

- -

- -

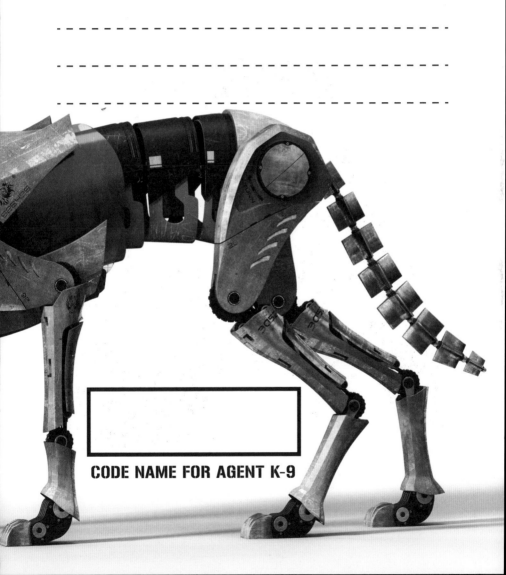

CODE NAME FOR AGENT K-9

CLASSIFIED: CASE NO. DX7

THIS PHOTO WAS TAKEN BY AN AUTOMATED HIDDEN CAMERA IN THE DESERT. GOVERNMENT OFFICIALS NEED YOUR HELP CREATING A SKETCH OF THIS BEAST.

9

ACCORDING TO LOCAL LEGEND, IT HAS 12 EYES, 2 ARMS, 6 LEGS, 1 EAR, 2 MOUTHS, 3 TAILS, & RAZOR-SHARP TEETH. DRAW THE MONSTER BELOW. GIVE IT A NAME.

POST THESE SIGNS WHEN CONDUCTING OFFICIAL AGENT BUSINESS. KEEP THE PUBLIC AT A SAFE DISTANCE.

SAFE DISTANCE

Hang to keep people out.

LASER TESTING

IN PROGRESS

DO NOT OPEN

Hang to keep people out.

ROBO-SHARKS

PROTECTED AREA

AT YOUR OWN RISK

SEND CONFIDENTIAL MESSAGES TO BROS

RIP OUT ➡ WRITE ➡ FOLD ➡ PASS OFF

USE YOUR
INVISIBLE RAY PEN
FOR SECRET COMMUNICATIONS, COUNTERINTELLIGENCE, AND DATA GATHERED WHILE UNDERCOVER.

TOP SECRET

FOLD HERE

CONFIDENTIAL

FOLD HERE

CLASSIFED

FOLD HERE

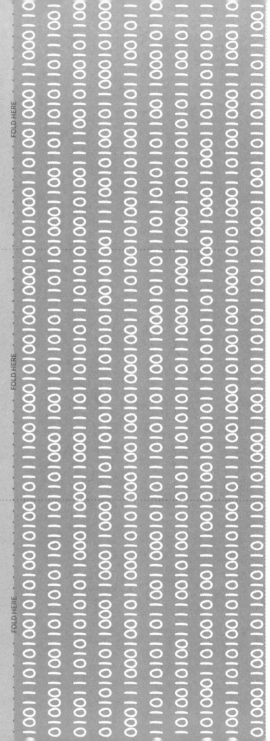

CONFIDENTIAL

CLASSIFIED

TOP SECRET

CONFIDENTIAL

CLASSIFIED

FOLD HERE

FOLD HERE

FOLD HERE

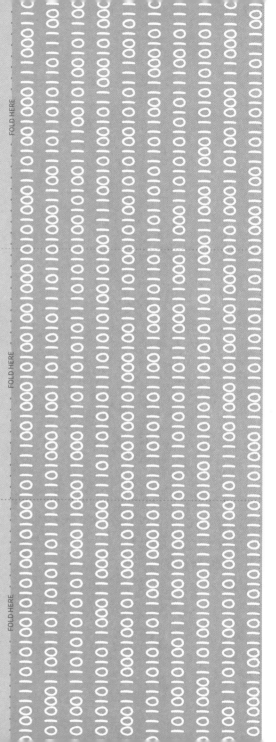

TOP SECRET

FOLD HERE

CONFIDENTIAL

FOLD HERE

CLASSIFIED

FOLD HERE

TOP SECRET

CONFIDENTIAL

CLASSIFIED

FOLD HERE

FOLD HERE

FOLD HERE

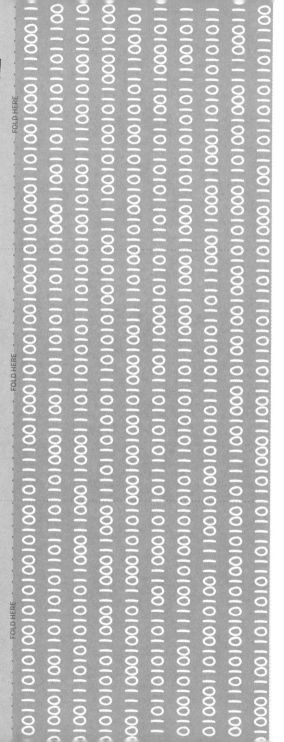

USE YOUR INVISIBLE RAY PEN TO ENTER THREE DIFFERENT LOCATIONS FOR DEAD DROPS

DEAD OR A LIVE DROP

SECRET LOCATION USED TO PASS ITEMS OR INFORMATION BETWEEN TWO PEOPLE. THE PEOPLE DO NOT MEET.

1. _

2. _

3. _

ENTER TWO OTHER LOCATIONS FOR LIVE DROPS

1. _

SECRET LOCATION WHERE TWO PEOPLE MEET TO EXCHANGE ITEMS OR INFORMATION.

2. _

LET YOUR UNDER-THE-RADAR BROS KNOW THESE LOCATIONS. THEN EXCHANGE SECRET INFORMATION, MESSAGES, AND PLANS.

TEAR OUT THESE GOVT-ISSUED FIELD NOTES WHEN NEEDED ➡

TOP SECRET · TOP SECRET · TOP SECRET

GOOD FOR SENSITIVE INFORMATION, COVERT PLANS, AND STRANGE OBSERVATIONS.

USE YOUR
INVISIBLE RAY PEN

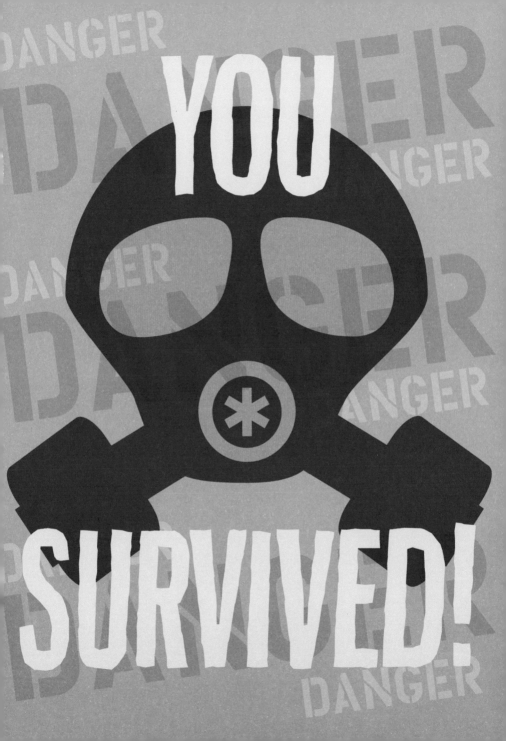